CORRUPT HEALTH SYSTEM & ECONOMIC RISE

While every precaution has been taken in the preparation of this book, the publisher assumes no responsibility for errors or omissions, or for damages resulting from the use of the information contained herein.

CORRUPT HEALTH SYSTEM & ECONOMIC RISE

First edition. January 15, 2023.

Copyright © 2023 Marina Kaubisch.

ISBN: 979-8215191644

Written by Marina Kaubisch.

WHO ARE YOU?

I am still standing

Personality and good intentions are your power. You act as the universe guides us. You are the red target.

This book represents the healthcare system through satiric pictures and examples from the actual cases that my coworkers and I had endured through the years. I'm talking about mental and physical terror, which ends in a long illness and even suicide. I worked as a nurse in hospitals across Europe where humanity and ethics choke under the financial exploitation of sick people and the middle class.

Can we operate peacefully without pursuing narcissistic strategies at the highest level? Does sincere charity exist in our non-profit organizations? You are not alone in fighting this impossible life task. I sincerely hope that you see how incomplete decisions shape the truth and our lives.

References USC Shoah Foundation

Holocaust Survivor: "Everything starts with words. Words have power. The words can bring you to Auschwitz

THE SYSTEM

What did you say?

Health Systems have a glorious hierarchy, which is not what we expect. More or less, it's a wrecked form of personal insanity mixed with libido issues. In significant hospitals, such leaders' components determine our life perspective.

In various minor editions, you will encounter three clusters in every Institution: Narcissists, sociopaths, and empaths. Symbiotic habitation from democracy and absolutism coexist more than ever.

Prominent leaders should be involved in this topic because their everyday decisions make a difference if somebody dies in the gutter or have a meal with his family.

What about Psychopaths? You never know.

INNOVATIVE LEADER

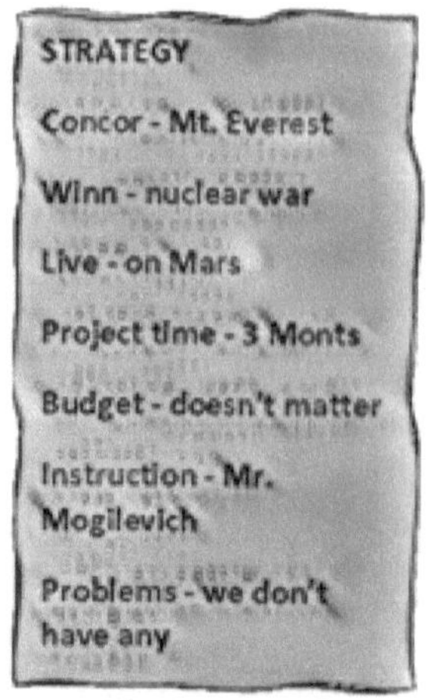

Flex the truth

Mr. Fox is never visible and forever busy. Ruffian's battles must resolve themselves because he never plays in the dirt. Foggy expenses are implemented into sophisticated strategies and are hard to digest.

With a fancy finish and immaculate beam, Mr. Fox doesn't take accountability for human lives.

Economic fact

Mr. Fox, are you playing the silent game? If you cannot bend your workers, you can bend the truth. Unfortunately, victim roles employees sink in self-pity. The urge to switch working environments doesn't exist. With this behavior, incompetent leadership and underpayment are acceptable and makeable.

Ethics

I don't know the sense of democracy. Why am I economically ruined if I tell the truth about incorrect behavior done to sick people? Am I an Outcast if I don't tolerate fraud? No. You are a sincere, brave, and incredible soul.

What can you do?

Tell the hard-hitting fact. The issue for you is not to be terrified of losing your job. Push through that hell. Your time is coming, and it will be great. Greater than losing your position or being a Hypocrite. Know that ultimate power belongs only to the Creator.

NURSING SYSTEM

Matrix No. 22340-52-779

Fiction or near future? Let's enjoy this ecstatic poem.

MATRIX

Hey Jim, I am Matrix. Welcome to psychiatrists. Hey, Matrix. I didn't know you exist! Oh, Matrix, you are everything I wanted. Oh, Jim, you won't be disappointed.

I am the best, and The Rest. Matrix, what do you mean? Are you the machine? Matrix, I am in love. I am a flame in this wicked game.

Oh, Jim, press the button, or this game will be forgotten.

The reality will slap us sooner than expected. Dehunmanisng work conditions are the leading cause for nurses worldwide to run and never return. Social stigma and hostility for those who care for their fellow humans.

If love and dignity don't count, what our trendy society desire in the future? The Matrix?

HYPOCRISY

I made soup. Would you like to try it?

Economic fact

Arnold is a senior physician who acts as the Hospital CEO.

He invents a unique saving method in the Oncology unit by reducing painkillers as much as possible.

High-tech treatments blend the dying clientele and are the playground for extra orbiter calculations. Behind the iron curtains, Arnold cuts the nursing staff, substituting them with medical students.

Ethics

I worked in this Oncology department. Being in a team of drained and unscrupulous coworkers, lazy to draw up and inject a vial of morphine, was unbearable. My Instructions were: " Painkillers only if nothing else works." I perceived cancer patients' hunger for mercy.

Terminally ill persons endure severe pain, misery, and depression. Going from one room to another, I distributed morphine to ease the tragedy I saw.

My crusade lasted one month. Group verbal attacks didn't surprise me, but something else. A verdict from Arnold hit me in the heart. "That's a waste of painkillers. They're all going to die anyway."

The savings budget was exceeded, and my actions were no longer desired. I wondered if Arnold would say that if his wife, child, or parents were in dying mode.

What can you do?

How will it be our last beat? We don't know.

Let us have mercy on each other and do the right thing.

BILLING SYSTEM

I am the modifier

Economic fact

The company has mandatory numbers which define different levels of care. Outdated billing systems need to be more transparent. How you treat a sick person is a mystery. Every sentence or action is adjusted to the annual balance.

Nursing scenarios determine the company's total budget and staffing ratio and perform as a leadership mechanism. Manipulating nursing records is a critical business model. In medical jargon, this is adjusting. This model of improvement always shines through. Who's right to say that any self-proclaimed billing system is the only one that can work?

Typical Situations in a home care institution.

Mary wants to eat alone in her room. This mental state is classified as anti-social behavior, and you already have a few thousand euros more in the budget. This is a dream- definition because it hits the highest points in care planning. And Mary prefers peace of mind. Everything is adjusted as it should be, and that's the guideline usually made by a single person. Behind closed doors, crucial accounts are "improved" wherever needed. Nurses are confronted with care planning, where they must write down the untruth. If not, they are expelled from the Institution.

The process of adjusting: Mary's whereabouts and illnesses he never had are meticulously listed. He is presented as a mentally unbalanced individual. Be aware of this crucial point – because the mental condition is the most difficult to prove, it brings many additional care points, which means money and prestige for the Institution.

Employees are drilled in a targeted manner. Brainwashing is carried out with all available means. Finally, these employees trade everything and everybody! CEO decrees the polished report to the health insurance company. Now, cash flows.

Internal, nonexistent expenses are covered, and battered elderly residents like Mary become zero. For them, each daylight is identical until Jesus shouts. Personnel keys and paychecks continue to weaken.

Ethics

You only get a foster home from the social welfare office if you are impoverished and ill. Suppose you have some savings be ready to hand them over and arrange yourself in the line of the famishing pack.

In such nursing homes, underpaid non-medical staff and greedy Management rule your life. The Chief is limited to solving self-provoked conflicts and collecting cash from health insurance companies.

What can you do?

Controlling and verifying this unscrupulous film scenario is nearly impossible. The Management shifts the blame to you. Don't sign what you can't be responsible for.

DIGIT

Who helps me?

Economic fact

Patients are digits on the monthly report. Balancing between living and freshly desisted ones obtains a financial boost.

Example of prolonging life by all possible mechanisms

Klara is 98, gasping for air, and unable to speak, eat or move. She is dying. She gets two infusions every day and is artificially fed. These costs are billed each month as a vital priority. The catch lies in Klara's last will, where she clearly defined her wish for measures that would not prolong her life.

Unfortunately, she no longer has a family, so in her case, the home's Management can decide with the doctor what is best for the nursing home and not for Klara. Imagine you have 20 females aged 80 to 98, and you can add up to 4 thousand dollars each month for each of them in your budget. Now imagine you are Klara, and you want to meet Jesus. What can you do? Nothing! You are a golden goose who will be "kept save." Life itself does not weigh this calculation system.

Ethics

As long as you are healthy, you overlook these issues. The perception changes when minor surgery obliges you to fib in a hospital.

You ring the bell seven times because of your dirty diaper and a stench that an animal couldn't stand. The pain is unbearable, but personnel doesn't have time to give you painkillers. Terrible, isn't it?

These are the actual circumstances that prevail in multiple clinics.

What can you do?

Act and set priorities. Remember Human dignity.

Don't allow affliction when you control the essential resources.

As a patient, pray that your sun may go home and forget everything wrong that happened to you.

Otherwise, stoically prevail in the unbearable pain: nothing and nobody can ever change ignorant and lazy stuff.

PERFECT TEAM

We made it

Economic fact

Perfect team members are a question of capital. Sugar and whip. Overpaid and denounced employees define the operative condition in successful companies.

Alone on an impossible project can be frustrating, even for the best of the best. Now, the conflict manager bombards you with feedback. The only plausible conclusion is that your emotions are a weakness.

How to satisfy your hungry Boss without being whipped? It doesn't matter what you do crushing is a well-proven discipline tactic. In a brief span, the perfect team is created. Everyone has an identical opinion. Nobody complains. The company has a success rate of 99%, resting on the wings of pressure and insecurity.

Ethics

How long can a sensitive person remain in this perfect team? If you don't play the game, prepare for long sickness and devastation. Eventually, you must exit this pit because of your self-respect.

What can you do?

Is it wise to accept the strategy of humiliation for bonus payment? Being able to settle the medical bill is slightly different from remaining healthy. Change is the only perfect constant.

BULLYING CREW

I think it was Micky

Economic fact

The chickens have limited eyesight. Nearly blind, how can they ever recognize a divine attitude?

Ethics

I labored in a clinic specializing in alcohol addiction. Three colleagues reminded me regularly of alleged errors I was supposed to correct. I took it peacefully. As I returned from vacation, 11 handwritten slips of paper were on my desk. Each report involved a different style of accusation. I took the "notes" and went straight to the CEO. To my astonishment, he desired to understand what had happened.

The next day, again, I got refreshed notes from identical coworkers. I tore it up in front of them and made myself clear that I would no longer tolerate this kind of bullying. I didn't argue or apologize. I photographed and kept the notes. In my mind, I was in front of the labor court. Did the CEO take it seriously? I'll never discover, but this case triggered numerous team member resignations.

What can you do?

Such groups are self-destructing. Is it worth fighting? Start your day with fitness and an excellent breakfast. Be content and grateful for the life you have. From time to time, you encounter a CEO who genuinely cares about their employees.

EMPATH

I am easy-peasy

You are the crying Empath, depressed, desperate, and isolated. What have you done wrong? You declared the fact and behaved rightly. Why is this so tough to comprehend???

Mr. Schmidt, the grizzly man with a big grin, revealed his successful son's anecdote. Mark had the same problem repeatedly. He needed help to grasp why his employees acted inconsistently, as discussed.

"Father, I speak respectfully and in simple words, and I'm sure everyone understood it. I pay well and have long-standing employees, but I can't dissolve these misinterpretations."

Mr.Schmidt: "My son, not everyone is like you. Most people can't think honestly."

What can you do?

It's allowed to be frantic. Feel it and let go. Defeats are stimulating to discover unique opportunities. Expectations are rotten eggs in a new basket surrounded by workers craving to crack them.

HEALTH   INSURANCE

I am a native Polish girl

Economic fact

Country law mandates health insurance by deducting unimaginable bonuses from one's salary. Health insurance companies can force and prosecute the working class in cases they can't pay. Now you are ill, unemployed, and without money but with health insurance that does not cover any costs because you are in arrears with your premium payments. And so the wheel spins for numerous revolted people.

Ethics

If you are seriously ill, you must give up everything you own to pay your bills. It is only a minimal percentage that the health insurance company covers.

After that, you are a social case, and this situation is more optimistic. Now the state must deliver deducted amounts from your pay. Of course, an 89-year-old lady also needs a hip operation and a C.T. scan. And this is what health insurance covers, and physicians must order! The hospital strategy is financed with these figures.

The family gets a beefy bill when the older woman passes, which starts the infinite court process.

It rarely happens that a physician in an E.U. country is convicted or has to pay damages. Negligent behavior is tolerated and covered up. There are no processes like in the USA. Physicians are an essential link in the System, who are tutored to type the proper declarations to fulfill a detailed budget.

What can you do?

With minimal health insurance in Poland, you can have the top treatment and enough money for everyday life. That is a rational, affordable product for the working class.

COST FACTORS

I need my manager tie

The Health system mercilessly punctures ethics under the pretext of goodness and grace. Who shows strength in crises where our ego is revealed? There are few fearless characters with this attitude. Bandages, food, or incontinence items are not even close to what a mocking atmosphere generates.

Our leaders are consciously not involved and silently accept an unbearable mocking environment, which is the fundamental reason for skyrocketing operating costs.

The corruption design is marvelous and self-methodical. Every month 2-3 work unsuitable coworkers are quietly bullied out. A self-proclaimed conflict manager steers everything in the right direction. Guilty is the human who dares to expose reality. His life's existence must be destroyed, removing him momentarily from his workplace.

Management's power games are not questioned. The vital issue is preserving authority.

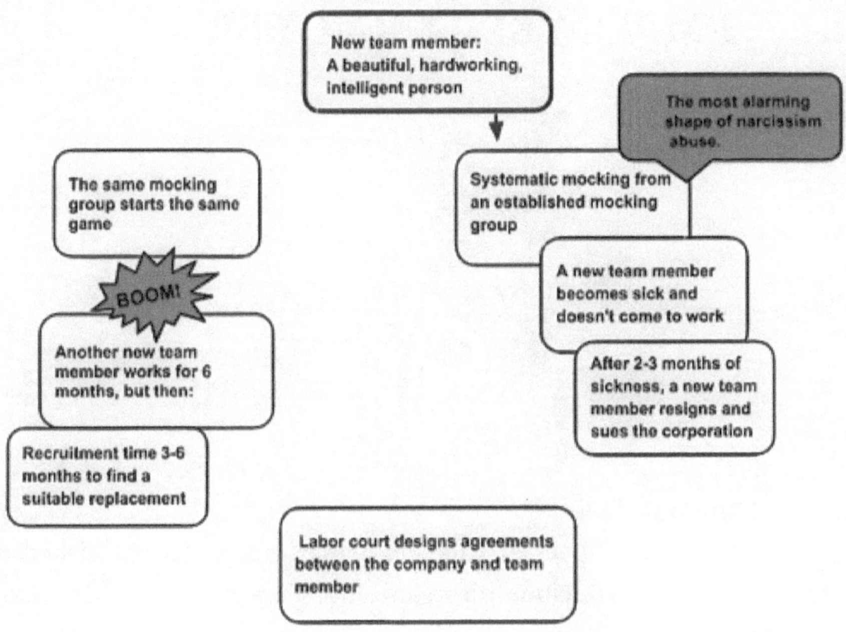

You don't need to study business administration to understand how the upper beats the lower. Take a tight gaze at this rotation. Why Is the turnover rate stagnating? Because of heinous bullying cases behind your Manager's back.

The situation repeats over and over again. The only unsuspicious employees are the mocking mob. Absolutely in charge, they work freely over time for the person they have been expelled. Which Manager doesn't appreciate involvement like that?

What can you do?

Act smart and minimize the cost with superb professionals and sovereign decisions. Keep the staff. Frustrated individuals in middle Management demolish your crew. The logical consequence is to change a department head with one with common sense.

Dear empaths, stay on the pedestal of honor. You don't need a revenge procession—evil deeds cracks by themselves.

EMPLOYEE TURNOVER

Let's see who stays

Economic fact

The crucial aspect of strategic planning is an unestablished team. Terror strategies include disorganization, unstructured daily routines, and awareness of how to run a social enterprise. It's always better to wrap everything up. Why?

That would imply an internal investigation, a shift of leadership, and a disgrace in the national newspapers. World Society thinks that we have enough nursemaids. This is switching and won't be more pleasing. In the future, dictators and their faithful slaves will exist. We won't have patients in today's constellation.

Those who spend can be fixed. The rest of us - nobody cares. The homeless, sick, and dead on the streets? The Middle Ages are catching up. Cholera, tuberculosis, and plague are lurking. The reason is our ignorance and indifference to each other.

In the future, it will be cheaper to take your own life in a specialized Hospital than be healed. Perhaps even free?

What can you do?

Do you make decisions? You are the master of the company. Ensure fairness to all players.

CONTROL OR TRUST

I control your mind

Economic fact

Control is better than trust is your motto! Reanalyze. A healthy corporation has healthy employees who want to stay. Spirit that my employees can achieve their work with a clear conscience brings serenity and sovereign conclusions.

The cardinal truth of not controlling anything on this earth is not in our minds. Who owns the world? A rich man? Surely not. Control doesn't exist, had never existed. The nature of life is flow. We are flowing with the air, water, animals, and each other. Flow is one unique constant of our existence. Control means planning. What do you want to design? The future of your company for the next 5 or 10 years. You don't know if you survived today! Today is the day to be a human. Only that. One simple human. Good, gentle, and just.

Ethics

Sustainability and long-term success are possible with people you can trust. Should lone wolf leave his job or be otherwise punished? These loners do an exemplary job and affect the whole company positively.

What can you do?

Pinpoint agitators with your inner voice and mindfulness. Don't paddle with mocking groups. You have the fuel to get everything back on track because you are a genuine leader.

DUTY OF CARE

today, I'm tidying up

Economic fact

In the employment contract, an extra clause describes what you must do. You are required to shuffle 48-hour shifts. You've signed. In the additional clause, you are not paid for overtime. You have to compensate for them as free time. This is a law jam. This technique exploits junior doctors mercilessly. For them, the unwritten rule is to whitewash unethical decisions caused by senior medics.

Ethics

Nurses have shared duties, working 10-13 days at a time, lifting patients over 100 kg without helping assets. Back-friendly work looks different. "Employees have to work kinesthetically," says the Management and giggles. This dishonest foolishness is an everyday routine in E.U. hospitals.

What can you do?

The employer's duty of care states:" In the employment relationship, the employer must respect and protect the team member's personality, take due account of their health and ensure that morality is maintained."

Scrutinize the legal code depending on which country you work in. Labor law is only sometimes favorable for the working class.

Collect the evidence. Write everything down with the date, time, and involved people. Be sure to know the doctors you were in touch with throughout the bullying phase. Make photos of working schedules, changes, and any ongoing extra services you are given. That is the reason for your inability to work, not your incompetence!

Be smart and learn the law. Eventually, you will know how to reach an affordable Lawyer.

DEATH AND LIFE

The feet need to be shortened

Economic fact

There's a brutal truth behind mortality. How fast can CEO reload empty beds to reach his 100% Quota? How many employees does he not need to achieve this Quota? What is the lowest pay? Mocking is a discipline strategy packaged as conflict management and communication.

Example

The palliative department is camouflaged under the name "Geriatrics and Rehabilitation." Dying is forbidden. This is crucial financial momentum and requires a unique tactic. There is a difference between keeping the person alive, having insurance pay for nonexistent cures, or letting the same person die peacefully. Do you want to be a successful manager? Change the header, and the world is yours.

Ethics

One spooky night shift in the geriatric unit.

9:00 p.m. Michael, 86, dead, with a smiling face.

11:00 p.m., Anamarie, 94, dead, still holding the Rosary.

2:00 a.m. Rosa, 74, dead, head left to the image of Jesus.

4 a.m. Valeria, 89, dead, with porcelain skin like a doll.

In a freaky state of mind, Dr. Janosh and I are wheeling the bodies into the morgue. This was the limit of my physical and mental ability. That night converted my life and pushed me to rethink my preferences.

What can you do?

Embrace mortality. It is the only way to live in peace! I documented each Patient's condition, which is essential and saves you from sadistic investigations. This is your weapon for staying healthy in a sick environment.

Get legal protection. Accept what you cannot change and leave before you get disgusted. Walking away is not a deficiency. Only a rare carry this internal strength.

BLOOD TRANSFUSION

I love you

Economic fact

Blood transfusion is an expensive affair. It will be even more pricey if you own a rare blood type. Unnecessary examinations, pills, and costly blood tests are prescribed to advance one's department. The intention is to charge exorbitant prices. The need is never questioned because it is arranged by the senior physicians who maintain endless Monopol.

Ethics

I asked my colleague which doctor ordered the transfusion. According to regulations, blood transfusion must be tested by the leading physician before I can provide it to the Patient.

"That's not necessary. Our doctors only work on the phone. You can give it." These were some of the answers that I received from my superiors.

I spent the next hour on the phone trying to determine which doctor made that verbal prescription.

Nobody took responsibility, and other colleagues were already wondering why I was examining all of this! My superior returned from his 30 minutes smoking break and said, "What else do you want, do your job." I refused to attach blood bags which made the case escalate. From a nursing point of view: I couldn't execute a nonexisting prescription.

"We always work like this." Just one of the delusion comments from the CEO. Because of a shortage of staff, professional incompetence, smoking rooms used as bullying offices, and physicians who don't want to be annoyed.

This example shows how to wipe out a human life through technical ignorance. So in style, "as long as it doesn't affect me, I'll act without conscience." Would you give your loved one a transfusion like this without a doubt?

What can you do?

Don't accomplish anything that you can't settle with your conscience! No matter how many people you encounter. You can report situations like these as "Critical Incidents." Will that transform anything? From my experience - no. In reverse, your reasonable behavior will be twisted and discussed with the Management during the smoking break.

CEO is introduced with smugged reality on the silver plate. You are now trekking in one of the most destructive styles of corruption.

I lost my job. Struggling for six months, I finally started somewhere else.

INFECTED WOUNDS
Suddenly everyone starts to save the money

I don't feel better

Economic fact

Nobody wants to admit that their company needs more bandages and qualified personnel to work due to cost-cutting measures.

Kata was an elderly lady in the Nursing home. She had a nasty wound on her leg and needed sterile dressing. After vacation, I returned to work, meeting Kata with a fever and delirium. He had an infection. I realize that the wound has not been bandaged for days.

I called an emergency doctor, and the resident ended up in the hospital because she contracted blood poisoning. The family was raging about the circumstances at the department and filed a complaint.

The Management communicated to me: " You react too emotionally. You are wasteful with materials, and everything doesn't have to be so sterile. You don't work economically and should consider the enormous costs we all cause."

I was butchered with lies by the CEO and the colleague responsible for this tragedy.

What can you do?

Sick people pay dearly for the services they do not receive. Do the job correctly and stay cool with a CEO whose only interest is their status. Ultimately, he will be swallowed by a more eloquent shark.

THEFT OF NARCOTICS

One more sip, and then off to work

Economic fact

Another sad truth we discover from the media. Everyone is outraged, and the deficient patients steal everything anyway. Such nonsense, isn't it? The strict rule allows only superiors or head physicians access to the drugs. Even as a nurse, you are obligated to confer before applying anything.

Drug Addiction Clinic. The young bully supervisor, Micky, slurps a liquid anesthetic Morphium. He would take a certain amount of fluid planned for the Patient and swallow himself.

If the Patient complains about not becoming his ratio, the answer is simple: "You are addicted, liar."

Marcel was a unique drug addict. He never forgets how many drugs he has become and knows that the supervisor is lying. CEO swept the incident under the rug. Marcel keeps up with his anecdote until external control fires Micky and CEO.

What can you do?

Check what is available and missing at the beginning of the shift. Be careful if your colleague keeps "forgetting" to hand in ampoules of morphine. Why is everything so necessary? False accusations can cost you the license to practice, and you'll end up as an "addict" even though you've done everything correctly. You will be blamed by people who have something to hide and are afraid of your sanity.

Trust your judgment when everything else dies.

FOOD

She stole the bread

Economic fact

Eating is perceived as something other than an essential conflict management tool. In this case, a single yogurt can save emergency doctor costs and police action. And in the end, that generates massive costs and holes in the budget - not a piece of bread.

Alcoholics have various daily patterns and schedules. Therefore, it is necessary to treat such patients so that no conflicts or other life-threatening situations occur. An essential part of this Management is also the food.

Since they are usually out late into the night, they must become meals later. Most of my colleagues believed addicted people deserve food at a specific time. Otherwise, they didn't get their meals. Circumstances like this lead to daily conflicts and physical violence toward staff.

As the Patient returned to the Clinic around 10:00 p.m. I gave him yogurt, soup, and his medication. My colleague saw this and got agitated. She planned to leave him hungry until morning. The addicted man heard her idea and was anything but satisfied.

This colleague did not realize that I had a tricky situation under control and calmed down a drug-addicted, hungry patient with this yogurt. The Manager refused to acknowledge my decision and lectured me about his tiny food budget.

What can you do?

Running a business free from bullying and constant conflict can be tricky unless patients get their needed nutrition. Addicted people are invisible, awkward, and unwanted in our culture. What about love and understanding? What could a man accomplish with one kind word?

Don't let anyone go hungry, no matter who you are! Consider your motivations carefully.

THE EXPLOITATION OF MINORS

"!"

Economic fact

Underage interns are employed as full-time workers in nursing departments under the camouflage of an internship.

Ethics

Mina, 21, is about to graduate as a nurse but prefers to kill herself. The supervisor has bullied her for months and given her the most demanding physical work to the point that she can no longer do it. He threatened her with a lousy internship certificate for her final exam. Propelling a young person to suicidal thoughts is an act of barbarity.

What can you do?

Would you like your child to get sick at the age of 21? Children are silent because they are afraid. Please look for dejected, sad faces and aggressive behavior in an otherwise tranquil child. Nobody wont to cope with frustrations in a lousy company. Get your kid out of this toxic environment. Mina moved to another Hospital and became her diploma as a nurse.

SKIN COLOR

Ethics

Akin, 23, from Kenya, was completing his paramedic training. His goal was to study medicine; with this job, he could finance his living. But there was one unconquerable problem. Management denied him everything he needed to complete this internship. After being blamed for: "didn't handle accurately," he was fired.

Martin Luther King was arrested and put into a police car with a shepherd dog. After two hours of ride, the dog sat on Martin Luther's lap. With noble character and high intelligence, this dog didn't look upon Martin Luther King as his enemy. What is interesting in this true story is how one animal treats and recognizes the righteous individual.

What can you do?

The best revenge is to finish an excellent education. Like Martin Luther King, follow your dreams.

YOU ARE FOREIGNER

His wife trains with a Cuban fitness trainer

I'll flatten you all

Economic fact

Underpayment for the top work and the top workers who have mastered international language skills and demonstrated many years of experience.

Highly educated employees from other countries are kept small without a solid option to work their way up. Management positions are reserved for locals who lick the System more than enough. For a well-established corrupt company, such people are a danger.

Accusing them of wrong communications skills, they are quickly mocked and repositioned. For decades such companies have kept making the same blunders and have exactly unaffordable costs, turnover rates of 99%, and juicy insolvency.

You speak 4-6 languages and maybe more, and you must apologize because you were born in Uganda. Your Swiss Boss corrects you in undefined german slang. Otherwise, YOU could give the wrong medicines. Foreigners are not expected to have perfect sentences,

M.S. Office skills and business background.

What can you do?

We are all strangers someplace on this globe. Conversing in different languages and meeting new cultures is excellent. It's enriching and prioritizing one's mental development rather than primitive judgments. Other points of view and different solutions to established problems are brilliant. Not even the most corrupt System stagnates forever.

THE NARCISSIST MAKES YOU SICK

Yay, I finally have time to breath

Economic fact

The hospital's CEO is a well-known, politically correct narcissist who has been slimming up for years. He uses a few other narcissists who have climbed up on him for years.

He gives them unlimited authority to flatten the little workers at the bottom of the hierarchy. In this way, the situation is secured in several forms. Every narcissist protects the other narcissist, and so it stretches into infinity. Narcissists are chameleons and appear in distinct variations of evil.

Manipulator likes to control work and people. He is a canny pretender who requires your trust. Wait until his selfish behavior reveals itself.

Energy Sucker gives you a feeling of tension and drags you down for no reason. If the others are optimistic, he's not engaged.

Pessimist lectures you repeatedly to feel worthy. Supports your work and, at the same time, rebukes every step you make.

Everlasting Victim desires prevailing pithiness and respect from others. Behind this mask is a demonic player who feeds himself from your optimistic energy. He will puke you out as soon as he finds other innocent lam.

Complimenter offers you false compliments or whatever you want to hear. In this way, he tugs you into his infantile world.

Ethics

A selfish person consciously and purposefully transfers his discontent and frustrations to the employees. This tactic is insidious and dangerous for your health because you have to face endless manipulations until it's final: «You are very aggressive.»

Countless working days and mixed shifts demolish you.

You endure physical complaints like back pain, tachycardia, and tiredness because you don't have time to rest. And that's why you can make serious mistakes because you're exhausted and can't think straight anymore.

What can you do?

You must have a deeper understanding of narcissistic behavior and practice it daily. It will be difficult but not impossible. I learned from online videos presented by astonishing Psychologists. After only two months, my life changed completely. I healed mentally and physically. For me, this was the best way.

How can you respond?

Powerful anger management: "I stand for myself." Tell this to narcissists calmly, respectfully, and firmly.

Be who you are.

Forgive. You have higher priorities instead of defending yourself against a deeply dysfunctional Person.

Irrelevance.

Patience. Wait and go slow. Narzisst is impatient, and soon you will catch Him.

Wenn narcist insult you try with this answer: "Whatever," "I am weary."

Psychiatrists call it: "Grey Rock." You don't do anything.

Self-care and love. Stay emotionally separated from people who make you sick.

Changing the working environment is crucial for your health.

MANAGER BURNOUT

I supervised cows on the alp. I know what I'm talking about
Economic fact

Masochistic behavior is compensation for one's failures and unfulfilled dreams. We see a human being with chronic fatigue and suppressed aggression. Black circles under the eyes, greasy hair, overweight. In slippers without socks, you see calluses on the soles of the feet.

As a stress reliever: a pack of cigarettes and cheap lighters wrapped between long red fingernails disclose - woman. Let's call her Greta. With yellowish teeth and a rough voice, she is in the category of cheaper Management. Would you survive one day with Greta? Let's find out.

Greta arrived at the department at 6:30 a.m., although duty starts at 7:00 a.m. Until other colleagues are there, he has criticized the tasks of night duty that do not appeal to her ideas. The night nurse has to stay longer and iron out the mistakes, resulting in overtime. The H.R. department officially approves this but pays nothing. The early shift arrives at 7:00 a.m. and meets annoyed and overwhelmed Greta, sitting at the computer struggling with the working agenda.

A qualified nurse calls in sick for one week. This nurse is working 12 days in a row. Now she was in bed with the flu.

Nursing Department has 36 disabled people and is understaffed at this moment. So Greta must step in, neglecting her actual activity, Management. Does it have to be that way? No. Greta can utilize a temporary team and solve this understaffing without tension.

Now we have one case of illness, one medical student, and thirty-six sick people without a leading hand. Greta orders the colleague from the night shift to stay and help out. The big bang happens at midday when residents need help eating. As you understand, one nurse cannot spread over ten pages. Greta begins yelling at residents, leaving them alone, and flees into her office. The weary nurse and the student are the only help for the elderly.

What are the Consequences?

The next day, Greta terrorized the sick colleague with dismissal if she didn't come to work. The result is a labor court hearing for Greta. The sick colleague never returned to work.

What happened to the nurse who was supposed to help out a little after the night shift? She also called in sick because she was in bed with a fever and back pain. The medical student was crying in the toilet, confronting his first nervous disorder. A group of relatives addresses a letter of complaint to local newspapers. The issue was described with one red title."Hunger and thrust in our nursing homes."

Greta is replaced with a more suitable manager who suffers from deep depression.

If this is only one day in the Nursing home, how does one year looks alike?

What can you do?

In case of overload, make an overload notice. Every company has it without speaking about this possibility.

Write down the occupation and daily routine like this and send it to the labor court with an overload notice.

SURVIVING ENVIRONMENT  **TOXIC**

I'll die for you, baby

Your Strategy

Combining these steps can bring you out of hell and make you stronger for every battle.

Learn the law - depending on the country where you live

Labor law, occupational safety, notice periods, bullying law, and an employment contract. You need to know how the law works and what steps to plan ahead of time. The law is always supreme. Read and learn these things because only by knowing what you have will you be able to make a difference.

Legal protection

You need adequate protection in labor court - before - the case hits. It means you can receive benefits only if the legal defense against this bullying case is settled for approx three months (depending on the country) in advance. It is an affordable sum for everyone. The best time is now. No matter where you work, you can use it. You will get a paid lawyer, all the annoying correspondence will go through legal protection, and you have any costs.

Write daily report

Date, time, colleagues on duty, and what you accomplish with whom. In the case of bullying, you have evidence for your statements.

Photograph schedules and all changes

The judge can see your working days and why you became ill. Split shifts or working 12 days at a time can benefit you if it is on this roster.

Psychologists or Psychiatrists specialize in bullying.

Catch one before things get urgent. Disability certificates determine the outcome of the court process. These doctors are willing to accompany you with particular knowledge and understanding. You are sick due to bullying. Bullying is why a written report from your psychologist or psychiatrist can do wonders in the labor court.

The notice period, E.U. Hospital

Complying with the statutory notice period and your sick days are crucial. Your employment contract extends by the days you are ill. But you can always do without it, and you don't have to pay it back either. Many employers take advantage of this ignorance and try to harm employees in this way. And this is the reason why you need a lawyer.

Submit written evidence to unemployment funds

Unemployment insurance doesn't care for you. Although your incapacity to work is indebted to your employer, the complaints will cause you to wait without money. Do it right, and don't get discouraged. Doctor's letters and sick notes are your golden ticket.

You have yourself

Are several sufferers also going through the same thing now? Unite and stand up for equal causes. If not, you always have yourself. Your life belongs to you. Nobody can tell you what you are supposed to do. Continue to do your thing correctly and independently. Despite your current misery, this to shell past.

New task

Education in Psychologie can save you years of suffering. Learn the line where crowds split, and corruption begins.

THE PSYCHIATRIST

I understand you, my child

Economic fact

The company doesn't want sick Employees. Being healthy and willing to obey is the primary urge. The unhealthy ones are the disturbance and cost factors.

Ethics

The company doctor requested an examination because I was sick for one month. My employer did everything possible to prove the opposite. For me, it was one exhausting game.

I went to this examination and told the doctor the circumstances that made me ill. I told the truth. Psychologists knew that certain things he must report to the labor court. I was glad that the psychiatrist acknowledged me.

It was an enormous struggle. I could no longer work anything. Developing severe heart failure, I take medication for the rest of my life

What can you do?

Have confidence in yourself and expose the facts. Everything that breaks you down and degrades you as a human is not worth your health! Who will care for you if you get seriously ill?

Is your family willing to care for you as you accomplish daily with your patients? Unfortunately, our reality is slightly different.

COURT TRIAL

At least I look sexy

Economic fact

Vast discrepancies that fire and establishes evil in humanitarian institutions are accepted and even applauded. The simplicity of communication makes the mountains move clear, crispy, and sincere words of truth.

I am innocent. Justice is on my side. How naive. The judge only cares about the evidence. And not every judge is equally sensitized to the words and actions of a bullying victim! That's where I see how our society covers everything up. The main thing is that our ideal world works as it has.

It depends on you what and how many you can endure without getting sick. If you know the legal steps and have help, you can disclose and fight for righteousness on your level. It is a good start.

We don't experience justice in our lives, especially the sick ones.

It was the first time management bullied me, lied to the residents and their relatives, and made everything pleasant, ignoring the pain of older people to save the painkillers.

Poverty is present. Not everyone can afford expensive medicines or better food. Shouldn't we all be treated equally?

I need to give poor people the same attention and tackle their illnesses as I do with everyone else. That's how the social approach functions for me.

Calm down, listen actively and stick to your evidence. Your employer will do everything to distract the judge from bullying. In my case, it was fictitious minus hours. The change in the roster would manipulate these hours during my illness. I was able to prove that, but the judge ignored it. I felt his arrogance and indifference. I was invoked for unfair settlement, which meant: paying back minus hours I didn't have

The judge wanted to know nothing about how these minus hours are made. His arrogance and indifference burned my belief in the Judicial System.

What can you do?

You are more than this situation. You're above this whole thing because you know: Universe is with you. You are the strongest person in that courtroom. Never forget that!

JUDGE

What is your name?

The democratic outcome in 21 st century

Who can predict the essence of the judge's heart? Prepare yourself for a surprising development.

In medical cases, we obey polished surfaces and facts that are lies. You dare to provoke Company's CEO with dirty facts about tottering excuses for the impoverished care quality and low personnel key.

The democratic decision in the 21st century is a thorny fighting process. What problems cause simple decisions to escalate to the level of impossible solutions?

We can take some lessons from the Lazaret system of the Crimean War 1853 - 1856. In Lazaret, Medical personnel was obligated to all wounded soldiers, friends, or foes. This military conflict is known as the first industrial war. But the soldiers are dying of epidemics and improper wound treatment more than bullets. Establishing a field hospital can be a wise strategic move, considering the reality we are trapped. It's time for "The Lady with a lamp."

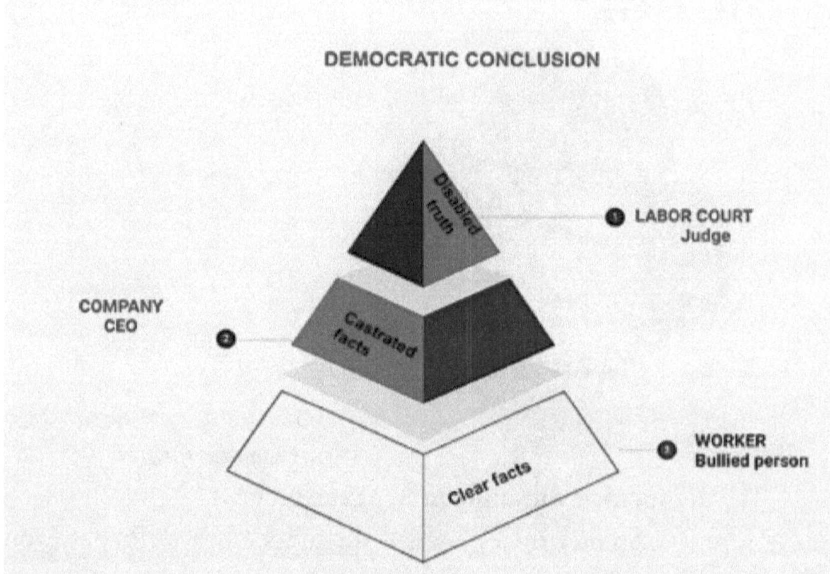

*Wikipedia

Florence Nightingale, 1820 – 1910, was an English social reformer, statistician, and the founder of modern nursing. During the Crimean war, Nightingale gained the nickname "The Lady with the Lamp."

FEAR

Mamma

Economic fact

Fear is power. Dispirited employees have no strength to complain about crooked decisions. Degradation among medical personnel is awful for those who cannot fit in.

Healthcare companies will do anything to avoid labor court. The court and the CEO ignore the duty of care that an employer must legally fulfill. The main idea is to punch disobedient ping-pong bools back into the bag.

Ethics

You are not isolated. Countless people can understand your agony. Lote of them has faced identical bullying cases as you. Have courage, take the first step and be what you are - a fantastic person who doesn't neglect the needs of the ill and poor.

I locked myself in my apartment, crying and feeling sorry. My heart was bleeding. I refused to ignore and tolerate evil deeds and unworthy behavior to keep my job. I refused to trade my soul for money.

What can you do?

Refrain from suppressing your intuition and emotions. Let it out.

Your health is your most precious item. Protect it. Pick up evidence from a psychologist and testify before the Labor Court. There is more than we know, and much is beyond our control. We can follow humbly and be there for the sick and suffering. We are all trivial piles of dust swept away.

EMOTIONAL INTELLIGENCE

Cheerio

Economic fact

Exploiting a person amid her immense misery is not a tribute to economic rise. Knowing how life will end for all of us should be enough motivation not to draw the last dollar from sick, needy humans.

Ethics

Mrs. Schmid was a patient with metastatic cancer and very busy. She is still working on her laptop, tinkering with her career, and the chemo infusion is dropping mercilessly into her System.

Her denial is expressed through shouting names, crying, and hating everyone alive. Material things are essential to her, but she needs - more. Even in the last days of her life, she humiliates and blames the medical staff for her unfair destiny.

Emotions, even hostile, are still emotions and should be perceived. Behind everything is a person who no longer sees or wants to see a way out.

Death was unacceptable to Mrs. Schmid, and she threw her anger at everyone near her. She was a private payer financially exploited by the hospital management.

What can you do?

The basic need for love and affection is in all of us. Recognizing emotional instability and anger and treating it with respect is not easy. People react differently; therefore, the concern is relevant to every life we encounter. Understanding sadness and helplessness is a strength and emotional intellect.

EMPLOYMENT CERTIFICATE AND HIDDEN MASSAGES

What a tangle

Economic fact

Personal vendetta, power, and humiliation are the means utilized. As a bullied person, you also get a confusing reference making it impossible to find a new job. You mostly end up being a social case despite having a great experience and correct behavior.

Ethics

Certificates are truthful statements about a performance in a field of work. Are the subjective opinions and formulated statements objective? No. What does this say about you and your abilities? Nothing. Superiors who systematically bullied you must write a testimonial about your performance.

What can you do?

Hidden statements are not allowed. Formulate the sentences correctly yourself and write a new certificate with the lawyer. In Europe, you have ten years for this! Don't just accept. You can also have your certificate checked on the free Internet platforms.

Buck up your rights.

LOBSTER FOR YOU

Or something else?

LOBSTER PLEASE

Oh, you beautiful lobster, how elegant you swim. You are so juicy. How can I resist? Waiter, please, two lobsters. Mak'it spacy for my wife, Tracy.

What is the price? 1000 dollars.How nice. I'm sorry, the lobster is gone. How is this possible? Lobster, please.

Honey, take a piece of cottage cheese. Oh, you beautiful lobster, I hate cottage cheese. Come back - please!

Acknowledge your best qualities and use them to bring love, light, and vitality into your own life and the lives of others. May clarity and peace replace confusion.

P.S. Be aware of guys in fancy hats and Cuban cigars. It could be the devil in disguise.

P-content-license-agreement

VectorStock Media Ltd (VectorStock, we, us, or our) provides a service for the supply and licensing of vector images, graphics, icons, and illustrations (Content) via the www.vectorstock.com website (Service). The Service allows people to contribute Content (Artists), to make their Content available on the VectorStock® website, and persons registered with us (**Marina Kaubisch**) to download Content from the VectorStock® website. The Service acts as an exchange to allow each Artist to grant to Members a licence to use the Artist's Content when downloaded. A person may apply to be a Member by completing the registration details on the Sign-up' page of the Website and clicking the tick box to confirm that they agree to the terms of this Agreement.

This VectorStock® Membership Agreement (Agreement) is between VectorStock and the person named as the Customer in your original registration to become a Member (you or your). Your use of the Service will be governed by this Agreement, the VectorStock® Website Terms of Use, the Take Down Policy and the Privacy Policy.

If any of the terms of this Agreement are inconsistent with those in the VectorStock® Website Terms of Use, the terms of this Agreement will prevail.

https://www.vectorstock.com/faq/member/membership -content-license-agreement#license-expanded

Don't miss out!

Visit the website below and you can sign up to receive emails whenever Marina Kaubisch publishes a new book. There's no charge and no obligation.

https://books2read.com/r/B-A-HZMW-QONEC

BOOKS2READ

Connecting independent readers to independent writers.

Did you love *Corrupt Health System & Economic Rise*? Then you should read *Underground Poetry - Pain*[1] by Marina Kaubisch!

For all of You lonely and disappointed Souls. Let's unite and be good to each other. Let's fight for our Hearts and beliefs. This is our time! Read more at https://marinakaubisch.wixsite.com/website-1.

---

1. https://books2read.com/u/bPN0Dz

2. https://books2read.com/u/bPN0Dz

About the Author

Working as a nurse for 20 years, I have issued my stormy adventures in one satiric approach. Today I am a passionate author, edithor, and pacifist. I hope I can touch your hearts to be compassionate and forgiving to one another. God bless you all. Marina Kaubisch

Read more at https://marinakaubisch.wixsite.com/website-1.

9 798215 191644